Dedicated to our children and grandchildren
both now and in generations to come.

First US Edition 2025

ISBN 978-0-9882583-4-1

Daily Audio Bible
PO Box 1996
Spring Hill, TN 37174

WWW.DAILYAUDIOBIBLE.COM

The Breathing Prayer

I have a small story
that I'd like to share.
It's about letting go—
it's the Breathing Prayer.

When I first
started school,
I laughed and I played,

but soon
all my worries
got in the way.

I felt very sad,
afraid, and alone.
I wished I could leave;
I just needed home.

With Mommy and Daddy,
I felt safe and sound.
But when they weren't close,
my fears came around.

My loneliness grew;
the days felt so tough.

But my daddy helped me—
he taught me some stuff.

He told me he wished
he could always be there.
He had something special
he wanted to share.

He wanted to teach me
something he knew,
something that he did,
and I could do too.

He said, “Close your eyes,
take a big puff of air.
Say, ‘Jesus, be with me,’
and He will be there.”

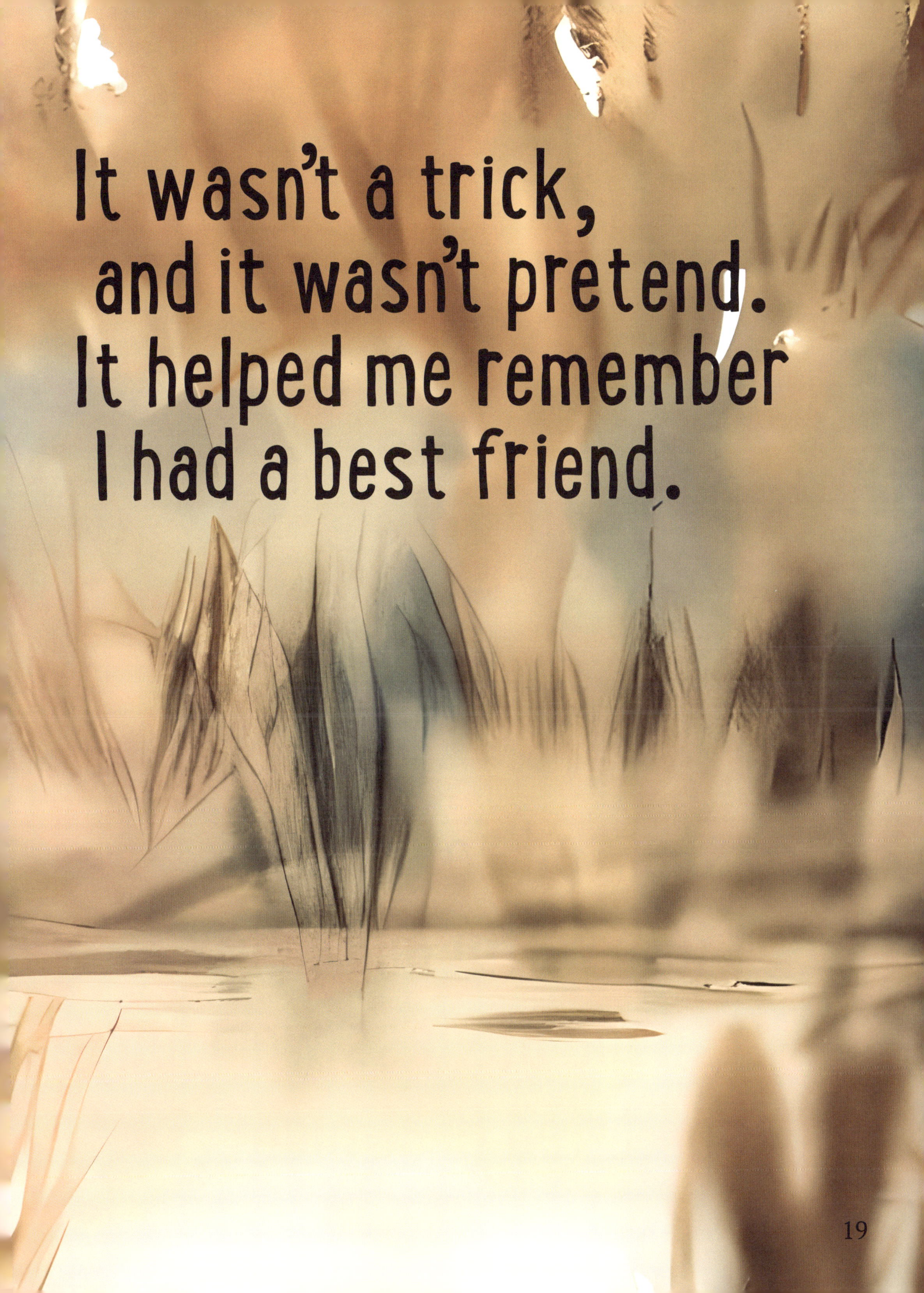

It wasn't a trick,
and it wasn't pretend.
It helped me remember
I had a best friend.

I started to calm,
I felt warm and light.
It made me less worried,
so I tried it at night.

Whenever I'm nervous,
lonely, or mad,

worried at school,
or just feeling sad,

no matter the reason—
no reason at all—

I know who is with me,
whenever I call.

It's not just for me—
this prayer is for you,
whenever you're lonely,
anxious, or blue.

No matter the place
and no matter when,

Jesus will hear us
again and again.

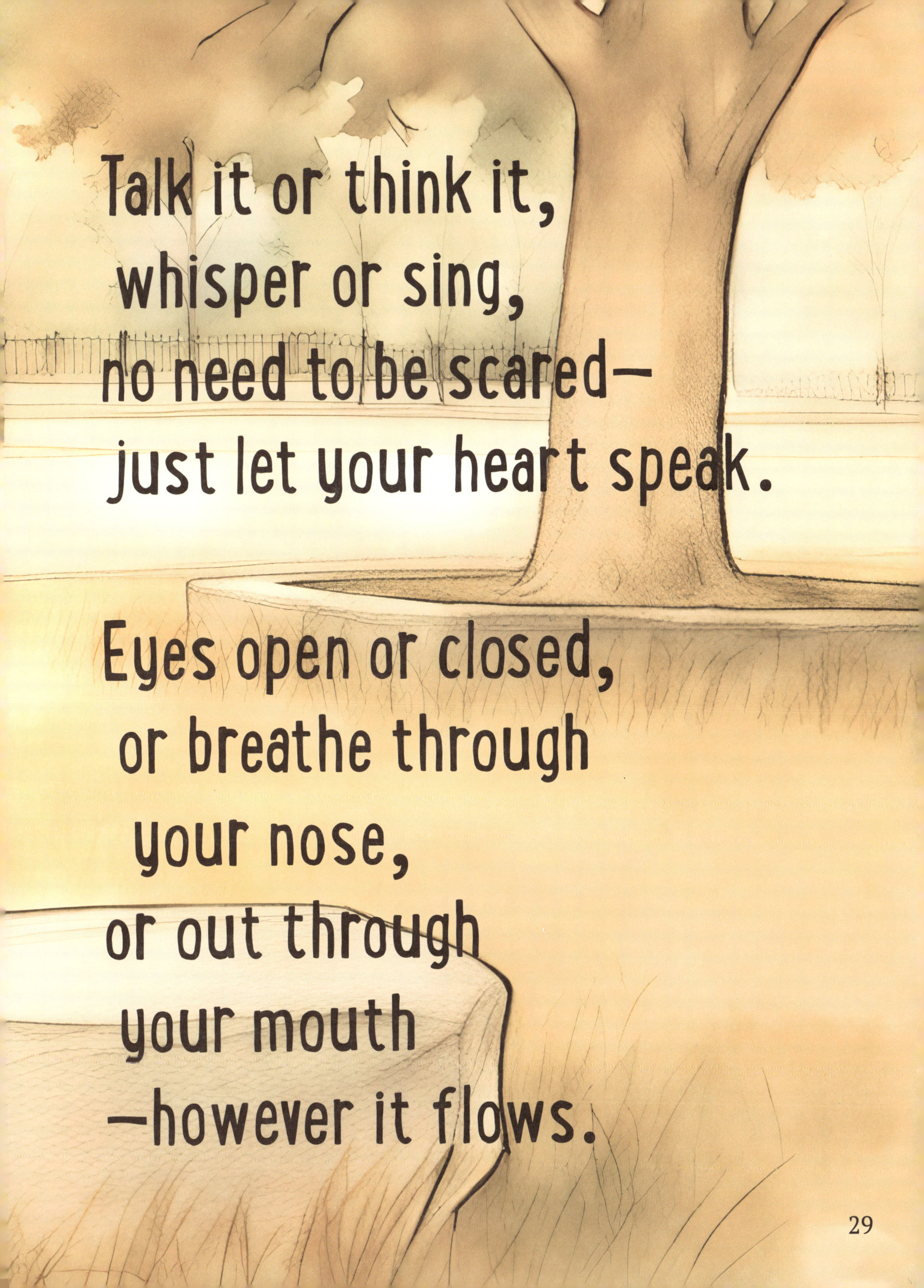

Talk it or think it,
whisper or sing,
no need to be scared—
just let your heart speak.

Eyes open or closed,
or breathe through
your nose,
or out through
your mouth
—however it flows.

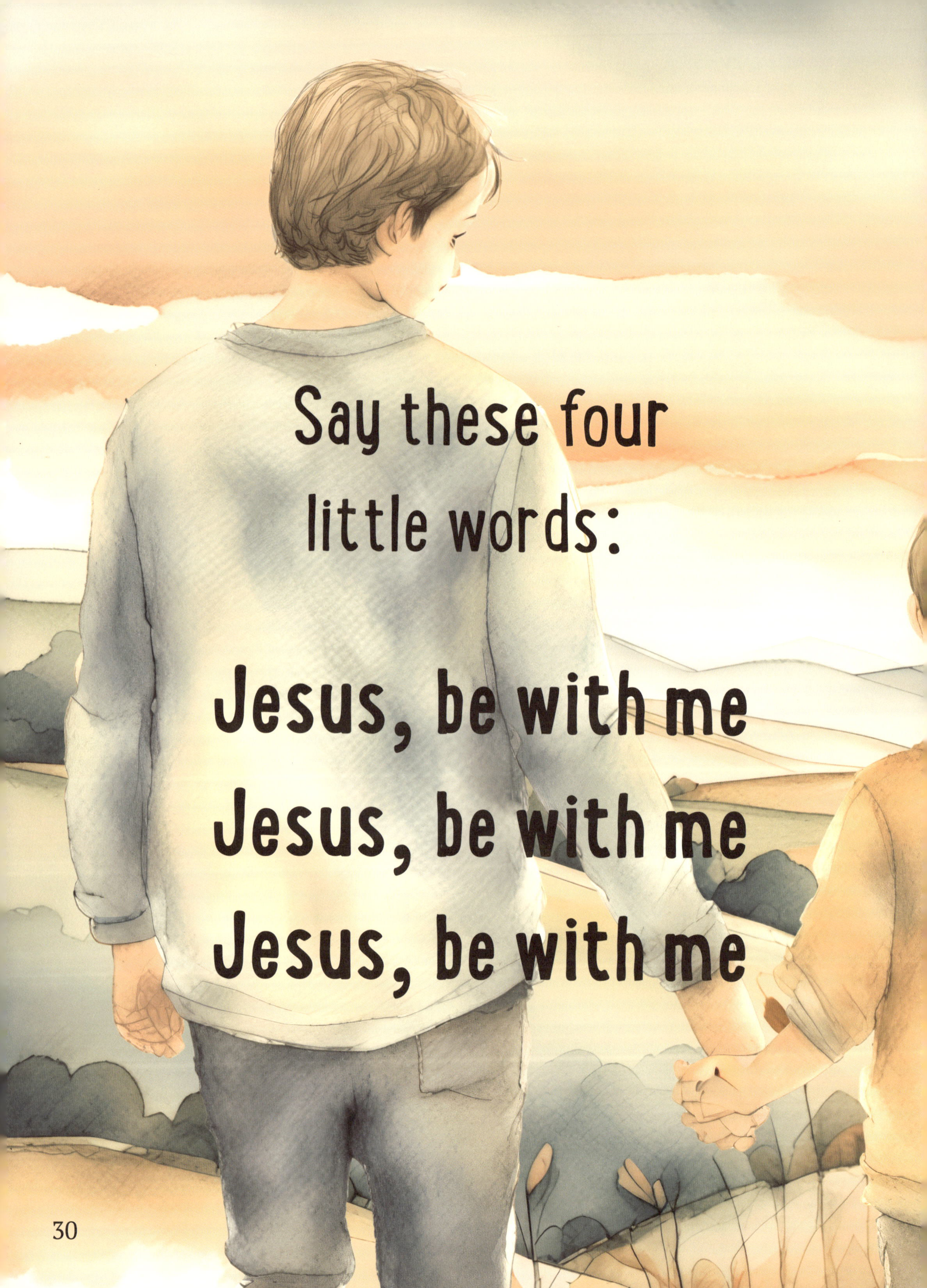

Say these four little words:

Jesus, be with me
Jesus, be with me
Jesus, be with me

You'll always be heard.

I hope this will help you,
just like it helped me,
to know God is with you,
and always will be.

Bee Thend.